CCSS **Genre** Folktale

MW00570349

Essential Question
When has a plan helped you accomplish a task?

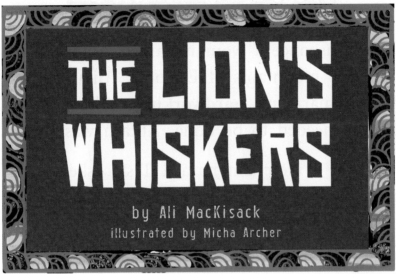

THE LION'S WHISKERS

by Ali MacKisack
illustrated by Micha Archer

Chapter 1
A ROCKY START

There was once a woman named Alitash. She lived in the mountains of Ethiopia. Alitash was kind and smart and **hardworking**. Whenever something needed to be done, Alitash was there.

One day, a merchant named Tesfa asked Alitash to marry him. Alitash said yes.

Tesfa had been married before, but his wife had died. He had a son named Dawit. Alitash loved children and was very happy to have a son, but Dawit was not happy. He missed his mother. Dawit cried himself to sleep at night, and he wouldn't let Alitash comfort him.

Alitash wanted to be a good mother to Dawit. She cooked his favorite meals and made him new clothes from fine cotton. But Dawit still wasn't happy and cried for his mother.

Alitash wanted Dawit to be happy. She also wanted him to love her. Alitash understood how sad he was, and she thought that love was the only way to heal his heart.

Tesfa was a merchant, so he often traveled for his work. As a result, Dawit missed both his father and his mother, but he did not want Alitash to comfort him in spite of his **loneliness**. Alitash began to think that Dawit would never love her.

STOP AND CHECK

Why is Dawit sad?

One day, Alitash went to see a wise woman in the village.

She told the wise woman her story and asked the wise woman for **guidance**. "Could you make a potion that will make Dawit love me?" Alitash asked.

The woman was silent for a long time. She stared into the fire.

"I can make you a potion," the woman said at last. "But first, you must bring me something very special."

"I will bring you anything you need," said Alitash, **assuring** the woman of her determination. "I love Dawit very much and want him to love me too."

"Then you must go into the desert and bring me three whiskers from a lion," said the wise woman. "The lion must be alive, and you must go alone."

Alitash gasped. She knew this was very dangerous.

STOP AND CHECK

What does the wise woman want Alitash to bring her?

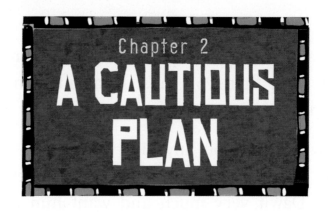

Chapter 2
A CAUTIOUS PLAN

Alitash couldn't sleep that night. How could she get three whiskers from a live lion? She tried to think of a plan.

Should she build a trap? Should she try to trick the lion in some way? Could she give him something to make him sleep?

How could she get close enough to a lion to take some whiskers?

But Alitash was clever and **determined**. She did not give up. As the sun rose, a plan was **emerging** in her head.

Later that morning, Alitash carried a piece of meat into the desert. She walked to Lion Canyon where a lot of lions lived.

She saw a huge lion lying on a rock. Alitash was frightened, but she was also determined. She walked toward the lion and stared at him. The lion stared back at her.

8

Suddenly, the lion stood up and roared. Alitash dropped the meat and **fled** quickly.

She didn't know if the lion was in **pursuit**, and she didn't look back. Alitash ran all the way home.

The next day, Alitash went back into the desert. She was carrying another piece of meat.

The lion was lying on the same rock as the **previous** day. This time, Alitash got a little closer before he stood up and roared.

Again she threw the meat onto the ground and ran. But this time, she paused and looked over her shoulder. The lion was eating the meat.

After that, Alitash walked into the desert every day. Each time, she carried some meat with her. And every day she got closer to the lion before he roared.

Eventually Alitash didn't run away when she dropped the meat. Instead, she walked away slowly and watched the lion eating. Each time she got closer to the lion.

At last, the lion let her stand next to him while he ate. Alitash knew it was time to see if her plan would bring the **outcome** that she wanted.

The next day, Alitash carried a small knife in her pocket when she walked into the desert. Her heart pounded as the lion walked up to her. When he began eating the meat, Alitash made her move.

She used the knife to slice some whiskers from the lion's head. The whiskers fell to the ground. The lion **snarled** and growled at Alitash.

Alitash leaped back. The lion snarled again and snatched the meat. He took it to his rock and kept eating.

Alitash picked up the whiskers. "Thank you, mighty lion," she whispered. "Now Dawit will finally love me."

STOP AND CHECK

What was Alitash's plan to get the whiskers?

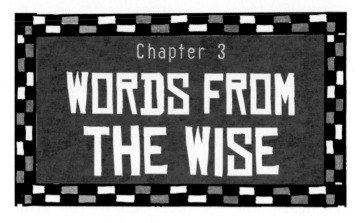

Chapter 3
WORDS FROM THE WISE

Alitash was excited as she cooked dinner that night. When she gave Dawit his bowl of food, she thought she **detected** a tiny smile from him.

"These whiskers have strong powers," she thought. "It seems they are working, and the potion has not even been made yet."

Alitash went to see the wise woman the next day. The woman looked amazed when she saw the lion's whiskers. She stared at the whiskers, then suddenly grabbed them from Alitash and threw them into the fire.

"Why did you do that?" cried Alitash. "I brought you the whiskers of a living lion, just like you asked me to!"

"You are brave and clever," said the wise woman. "You do not need a potion. By getting the lion's whiskers, you proved that you already have what you need for your stepson to love you."

"But I don't understand," said Alitash.

The wise woman looked at Alitash, "You do not need a potion to win your stepson's love," she said. "Tell me how you got these whiskers."

"First, I thought of a plan to get near the lion," Alitash said.

"And how did you come near the lion?" the wise woman asked.

"Slowly, with **patience** and respect. I didn't get upset about how long it took me," said Alitash.

"Why do you think your plan worked?" asked the wise woman.

"I followed my plan, and focused on my **goal**."

"And why did you continue with your plan?" the wise woman asked.

"Because I love Dawit," Alitash said. "And I want him to love me."

"So you already know how to win the boy's love," the wise woman said. "Treat him with patience and respect like you did with the lion. Go slowly. In time, the boy will learn to trust you, just like the lion did. Love will come if you are patient."

Alitash left the wise woman's hut without a potion. But she had a new understanding about love. She felt **gratitude** for the wise woman's help.

Alitash thought about the wise woman's words. And slowly Dawit and Alitash grew closer.

One day he asked her to make him some clothes for a party. She smiled and thought of the day when she cut the lion's whiskers. Alitash knew that one day Dawit would love her as much as she loved him.

STOP AND CHECK

What happened when Alitash took the whiskers to the wise woman?

Summarize

Use the most important events from *The Lion's Whiskers* to summarize the story. Your graphic organizer may help you.

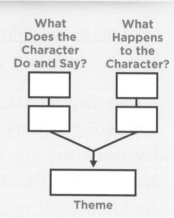

Text Evidence

1. What is the theme of *The Lion's Whiskers*? How do Alitash's actions support the theme?
   THEME

2. What does the word *paused* mean on page 9? Use context clues to figure out the meaning.
   VOCABULARY

3. Reread page 15. Write about Alitash's actions with Dawit at the end of the story. How do her actions support the theme?
   WRITE ABOUT READING

Compare Texts
Read about the steps in a process that lead to a very useful product.

From Fiber to Fashion

In *The Lion's Whiskers*, Alitash makes clothes for Dawit from cotton.

Cotton grows on a plant. To make cotton into cloth, the cotton is picked. It is then cleaned, spun into thread, and made into cloth. In the past, this was done by hand.

1. Growing Cotton

The cotton fiber forms inside the seed head of a cotton plant. The seed head is small and round. It opens when the seeds are grown.

Cotton grows in the seed head.

17

Today, machines pick cotton. The machines use air to blow the seed heads into a bin. Then the cotton seed heads are taken from the field to the factory.

2. Processing the Cotton

At the factory, the cotton is put into a machine called a gin. The gin takes out dirt, stems, and leaves. It also pulls the fibers from the seeds.

Now the fiber is called lint. The lint is cleaned, and the short fibers are removed.

Then the lint goes into a machine that combs the fibers. This straightens the fibers and forms them into a soft rope. Combing the fibers also makes sure that all the dirt has been removed.

Machines made processing cotton much easier.

3. Spinning and Weaving the Cotton

A spinning machine twists the rope into yarn. The yarn is threaded into a weaving loom or a huge knitting machine. A loom weaves a large, flat piece of fabric. A knitting machine makes a big tube of cloth.

Cotton goes through many different steps to become cloth.

Then the cloth is bleached and dyed. Sometimes the cloth is printed with designs. After that, it is ready to be cut to make clothing or other things.

Make Connections

What are the steps to change cotton into cloth? ESSENTIAL QUESTION

How do *The Lion's Whiskers* and *From Fiber to Fashion* both show how steps can help achieve a goal? TEXT TO TEXT

Focus on Genre

Folktales Folktales are stories that were first told out loud long ago. Most folktales have a character who must meet a challenge or solve a riddle to win a reward. Actions and words may be repeated.

Read and Find

- The story begins "There was once a woman ..." This sentence tells you that it is an old story (page 2).

- On page 5, the wise woman gives Alitash a challenge.

- On page 10, Alitash walks into Lion Canyon every day.

Your Turn

Work with a partner. Think of another folktale you know, such as "The Three Little Pigs," "Goldilocks and the Three Bears," or "Little Red Riding Hood." Discuss the characters and the plot. Explain to the group why the story is a folktale.